I.T. ESSENTIAL HELP GUIDE

ZORTEX LTD

TABLE OF CONTENTS

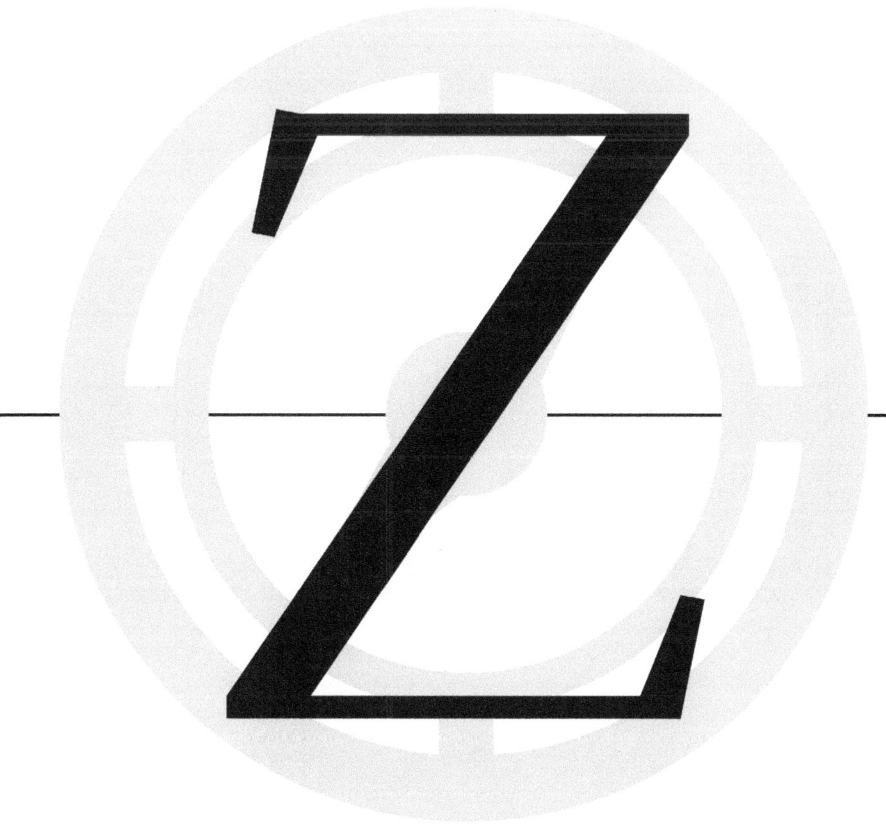

WELCOME!

Thank you for purchasing our I.T. Help Guide! Hopefully, you learn a few things that can help you out with some computer knowledge.

With a world that is revolving more and more around technology, it's important that we can keep up with it all. Most of the time it can feel like we've got it under control but sometimes, we can come across problems. They can be something major or they can be something little but annoying. Either way, when that happens, it's incredibly frustrating.

This guide is aimed to give you some general advice on some common computer issues that you can fix yourself. Hopefully, you'll find it helpful to have something handy when you come across an issue.

It also provides some shortcuts that can help you in day to day computer processes such as word processing, browsing the internet, etc. You may not need all of them but it can be useful to have them around and see if they can speed up your day.

FAQ'S

COMPUTER WON'T TURN ON

Firstly, it may be obvious but make sure it is plugged in. If it looks plugged in, give it a little push to make sure that the plug is fully connected. Check the other cables as well. Make sure the power cable is properly connected to the computer and that the computer is connected properly to the monitor and that the monitor is plugged in.

If you're on a laptop and the computer itself is on, make sure that the screen is switched on (one of the function keys usually has a little screen symbol). For a desktop monitor, the power button is usually somewhere on the bottom right.

COMPUTER IS FROZEN

Try right-clicking on the application on the taskbar that is frozen and select close. If you can't click, try opening the task manager using the keyboard shortcut and closing all the applications. You could also try to shut it down using your keyboard ('Ctrl' + 'Alt' + 'Delete' may bring up options so you can try to shut it down using the tab key until you reach the shutdown icon).

If you literally can't do anything, press and hold the power button for a few seconds (please note, this means you will most likely lose anything that you didn't save and it's not great to turn your computer off this way). If all else fails, you can unplug it and plug it back in again, but this also isn't great for your computer.

FAQ'S

COMPUTER IS SLOW

It may be clogged up with lots of application information that you aren't using. The best thing is for you to go through all of your installed programs (Start -> Control Panel -> Programs and Features). Right-click on an application to uninstall it but make sure it's something that you won't want to use or have anything that needs it to run. If in doubt, leave it for the time being. You can also use the installed Defraggler. Open up the Start Menu and then type in 'defrag' and select 'Disk Defragmenter'. Select 'Defragment Disk' and leave it running.
Another point to mention is to make sure what your PC specifications are. Not every computer has the capability to run all software so it may be the case that you are asking too much of your PC. Take for example you have a computer with an i3 processor but you are trying to run Adobe Premiere Pro (video editing). It won't be able to cope.

INTERNET IS SLOW

The easiest thing to do is just restart the router. There is usually a button on the router that allows you to restart it, so press and hold that for 5-10 seconds and it should hopefully speed back up once it starts working again. You can also switch off the power to it for 10-15 seconds which should also improve the connection.

If your wireless internet connection isn't very good, you can buy a wireless powerline adapter which will give you a stronger internet connection. One cable and adapter will plug into the router itself and the second will plug into whatever device you need (i.e. PC or games console). It's a great way to have a constant and stronger speed.

If wireless internet is important to you (say your device doesn't have an Ethernet port), you can buy WiFi boosters which connect to your network but only need to be plugged into a mains outlet.

There are different internet bandwidth speeds that are provided by your internet provider. If you have a router that only offers a smaller bandwidth (such as 5Mbps), you may notice that certain websites don't run well. Equally, if you have a number of devices connected to a router, you will need the bandwidth capacity to provide the same internet strength to all of those devices. If you're unsure about the internet speed you have, you can use an online speed checker and then speak to your internet provider to see if they have something more suitable for your requirements.

FAQ'S

LOST FILES

If a file has disappeared but you have recently used it, open your file explorer, and select 'Recent Places' which should be on the left-hand side. A list of all your recent folders or documents will appear so have a look through there. Ultimately, you can run a search in the file explorer for the title of the document. Either search throughout the whole PC or if you know a folder that it should be in, search in there. If it is a Word or Excel document, you can open up those programs, go to 'File' then 'Open' and hopefully the title of your files (if recently used) should be there. Also, check the desktop recycle bin.
Prevention is key here so if you can, try to back up important files. The cloud is ideal (use a free service such as Google Drive) since you don't need to store it on a physical medium but you can also access it on any device (meaning ports aren't an issue). Uploading to the cloud also means that the most recent version will always be accessible rather than trying to remember which USB memory stick the files were saved to. However, USB drives can be more favourable as a tangible item and not having to pay a subscription fee should you need more space.

HOW TO CLEAR COOKIES

In the browser, go to the menu (sometimes three dots) at the top of the page, select more and then 'clear browsing data'. This will open a new window and a pop-up that will give you the options to clear your internet history, the cookies stored, and the cached data. You can also set your cookie preferences on individual websites and since the GDPR legislation, you can decline the use of cookies on most sites. There are instances where there are necessary cookies (i.e. for online shopping), but you can set your preferences with cookies to prevent advertising cookies from being stored.

BATTERY IS DRAINING QUICKLY

Your battery may be draining quickly because too many applications are being run. Try not to open too many things at once and close applications once you've finished with them. Laptop batteries may drain quicker if the laptop is hot or overheating. If you plan on using it a lot, maybe invest in a laptop fan which will help keep it cool and hopefully improve battery life. It is also possible to ruin some battery types by 'overcharging'. Most batteries now are created to prevent this, but it is worth making sure your laptop is not plugged in once at 100% and also not to let it drain completely.

KEYBOARD SHORTCUTS

MICROSOFT OFFICE

- To launch spell checker, press 'F7'
- To launch thesaurus, press 'Shift' and 'F7'
- To refresh a webpage, press 'F5'
- To select all in a document, press 'Ctrl' and 'A'
- To make text bold, highlight the certain text and press 'Ctrl' and 'B'
- To make text italic, highlight the certain text and press 'Ctrl' and 'I'
- To underline text, highlight the certain text and press 'Ctrl' and 'U'
- To copy text or image, press 'Ctrl' and 'C'
- To cut text or image (copy it and remove it from the area), press 'Ctrl' and 'X'
- To paste the last copied item, press 'Ctrl' and 'V'
- To search a document, press 'Ctrl' and 'F' which launches the 'Find' dialogue box
- To make a new document, press 'Ctrl' and 'N'
- To open a document, press 'Ctrl' and 'O'
- To save a document, press 'Ctrl' and 'S'
- To print a document, press 'Ctrl' and 'P'
- To redo the last action, press 'Ctrl' and 'Y'
- To undo the last action, press 'Ctrl' and 'Z'
- To change which app/screen is open, press 'Alt' + 'tab'

Note: on Mac, it is usually the same shortcuts but using 'cmd' rather than 'ctrl'.

WINDOWS

- Open the task manager, press 'Ctrl' and 'Shift' and 'Esc'
- To switch sticky keys on or off, press 'Shift' five times
- To open the start menu, press 'Ctrl' and 'Esc'
- To change your screen orientation, press 'Ctrl' and 'Alt' and the arrow key for which way you want the screen to be.
- Pressing the Windows key and 'M' to close all of your open programs
- To view browsing history, press 'Ctrl' and 'H'
- Press the 'PrtScn' button to take a screenshot of your computer. This can then be pasted into a document. (Sometimes one of the function keys may need to be pressed on some laptops)

MICROSOFT EXCEL

FORMULAS

- To get the total of a series of numbers: =sum(X:Y)
- Profit Margins: =(X-Y)/X
- Minimum Value of a set of data: =min(X:Y)
- Join multiple cell data: = CONCAT(X,Y)

CONDITIONAL FORMATTING

- Highlight cell or cells you want to use for conditional formatting
- Open the 'Home' tab
- Select 'Conditional Formatting'
- Hover over 'Highlight Cell Rules'
- Select 'Greater than'
- Input the value you want it to be greater than (i.e. above zero)
- Select the colour style
- Go to manage rules to edit or add another rule to the highlighted cell

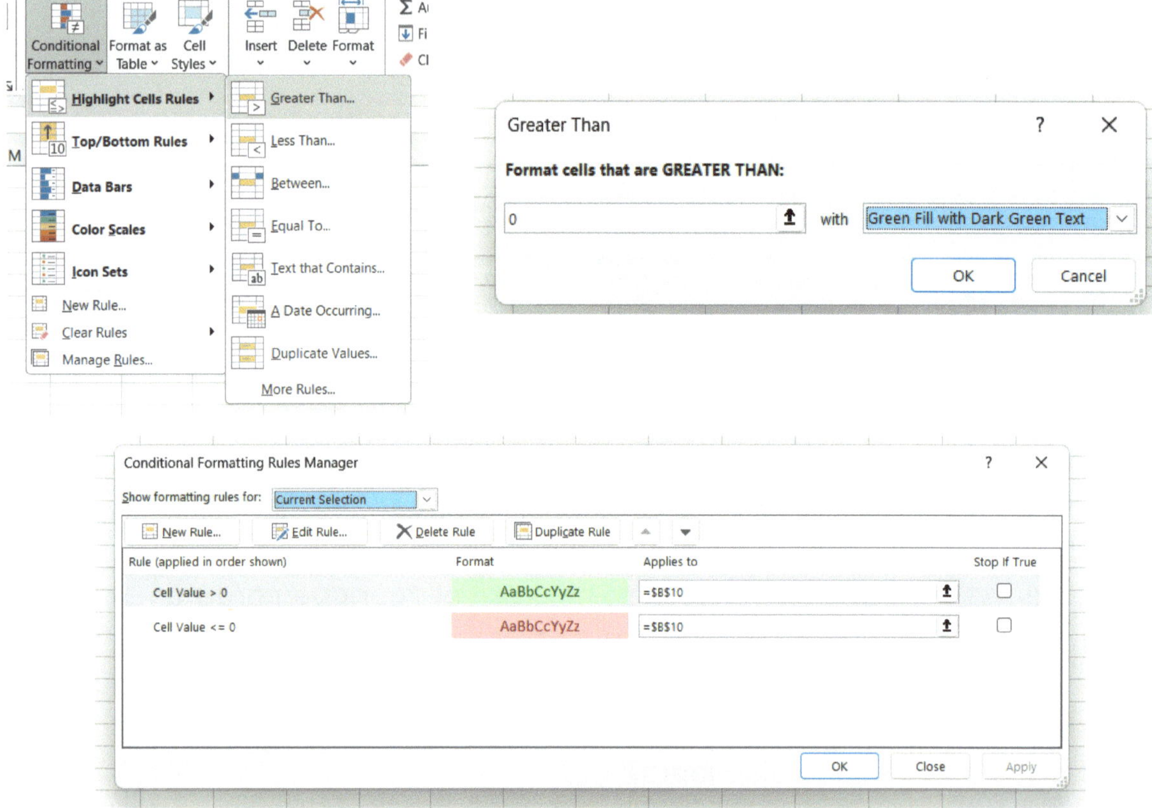

KEY TERMS

- **CPU** - Central Processing Unit. This is the main hub of the computer. It's the brain. It processes all of the data along with the instructions that are given to it. Intel is a common manufacturer of CPUs. For example, they have i7-11th Gen which would be a more powerful processor than i5- 11th Gen.
- **GPU** - Graphic Processing Unit. This is the part of the computer that renders the images you see on screen. If you're playing games, you will need a more powerful graphics card. A couple of examples of big brands for GPUs are Nvidia and AMD.
- **RAM** - Random Access Memory. This processes all of the current tasks that are going on. It is a type of memory but it is for storing current information that you can access quickly. For higher level tasks you would want either 8GB or 16GB RAM.
- **OS** - Operating System. This is what runs your PC and the software installed on it. Examples include Windows, Linux, and MacOS.
- **SSD** - Solid State Drive. A type of storage. Because of the way it is built, it is less susceptible to damage, hence the higher price point.
- **HDD** - Hard Disk Drive - This is an older form of storage which is still good but as the internal components are not solid, it can be damaged more easily than an SSD. They are cheaper though so are still present in lower-priced PCs.
- **FPS** - Frames Per Second. This refers to the frame rate that a PC is capable of. Most movies are filmed in 24fps however, you want your PC to be capable of displaying 60fps or at least 30fps.
- **HD** - High Definition. The quality of the display.
- **UHD** - Ultra High Definition. A higher quality of display than HD.
- **Port** - Inputs such as USB, SD, etc. When looking at PCs, you want to be aware of the ports it has available. If you do photography, you would want an SD card slot. If you use USB flash drives regularly, you would want to make sure it has USB slots. If it has USB-C ports, you may consider purchasing an adapter or a hub with other types of ports such as HDMI. Finally, you'd also need to consider if you need an ethernet port if you want to be able to connect to a network through a cable rather than via WI-FI.

TECH TALK

- **AI** - Artificial Intelligence. Computers that are designed to take in a lot of information and learn from it, allowing users to receive bespoke assistance from a machine.

- **Backlinks** - a link from an external website to a specific webpage.

- **Cookie** - a small amount of data generated by a website and saved by your browser.

- **DHCP** - Dynamic Host Configuration Protocol (usually assigns an IP address).

- **Firewall** - can be either hardware or software. It has a series of rules to monitor and allow or reject access from the internet onto your machine or internal network.

- **FTP** - File Transfer Protocol, transferring files over the internet.

- **IP Address** - Internet protocol, a specific and unique address for a device on the internet or a local network.

- **ISP** - Internet Service Provider.

- **POP3** - Post Office Protocol. A standard method of delivering email messages.

- **PoE** - Power over Ethernet. Some devices can be powered by an ethernet cable, but that could mean a switch with PoE capabilities is necessary. For example, an office that uses 'voice over cloud' phones, would benefit from being connected to a PoE switch, and then powering the PC and phone from the switch directly.

- **SEO** - Search Engine Optimisation. A series of techniques (such as the use of keywords) allowing a higher quantity and better quality of traffic directed to a website/webpage.

- **SSL** - Secure Socket Layer. A protocol for sending information securely over a webpage (the symbol is a padlock at the left of the web address bar).

- **URL** - Uniform Resource Locator. The web address for a website that is entered in the address bar.

- **VPN** - Virtual Private Network. A secure service that allows you anonymous access to webpages through "tunnels".

TIERS OF TECHNOLOGY

TIER 1

This is the most basic tier of technology but it's perfect for if you only need to use technology to complete simple tasks. If you're looking at PCs, it would mean that you don't need a lot of RAM or SSD storage. It's a lot more budget-friendly and it's unlikely you would notice a big difference.

If you're looking at phones and tablets, providing you don't plan on using them like a computer, you can go for a pretty basic model. It will still have a lot of capabilities if it's a smartphone, but it won't cope as well if you try and use memory-intensive apps.

Price Point = £400 or less

TIER 2

This tier of technology is perfect for if you want to delve a little deeper into computing. You may want to make your own promotional material or you may want to experiment with some other software. This is the most common tier as for the majority of people, the specifications of computer technology in tier two allow for flexibility and the use of common software.

There are some downsides; one being that it can still be quite costly but not be powerful enough if you want to use more professional software. If you wanted to do video editing, a mid-range PC would most probably crash as it won't have enough RAM and the GPU will be a lower specification.

If you're starting your own business and you just need a computer, or you need a computer for work, then this tier should be sufficient enough for you.

Price Point = £400 - £1000

TIER 3

This tier is where the top-spec computers are. They have the most capabilities but they also come with the most expensive price tag. These computers are built to perform difficult tasks such as video editing, image manipulation, gameplay, etc.

For an average user, they will not get the full experience out of one of these PCs; they are more likely to notice that it just runs faster. At least that means whatever task you want to do, the computer won't be the reason to slow you down.

If you are a digital creator or need a PC to offer full flexibility, it is worth investing in a machine from this tier as it should last you a good few years and it won't leave you wanting.

Price Point = Over £1000

HOW TO CLEAN YOUR PC

It is advised that you physically clean your computer every 6 months to a year but you don't really need to clean it unless it is having cooling issues. If you don't need to clean your PC then I wouldn't as it isn't worth potentially ruining some of the components. If you think it needs cleaning but are not confident in it then you can send it to a tech company who should be able to do it for you. However, if you want to clean it yourself, here are some steps below:

- Purchase an Air Duster (you can usually get them pretty cheap from places like Poundland and they are just as good as the more expensive ones)
- Unplug all the cables from your PC and place it on a table of some sort if not already (and you may want to do this in a well-ventilated room as it can get dusty)
- Unscrew the side panel off of the PC (making sure not to lose them) and gently slide off the panel
- You can use a microfibre cloth to get off any big bits of dust but personally, I prefer to use an air duster for all of it
- Use the air duster in short spurts to clean each section of the PC making sure that it isn't too close
- Sometimes, the compressed air can come out with a bit of water so before going straight in, test it away from the PC as you don't want to get water on the circuits
- Once done, wipe any big bits of dust away from the bottom of the PC, slide the panel back on and put the screws back in place

HOW TO CLEAN YOUR PC

There are of course some prevention methods:

- **Don't** put your PC directly on the floor or on carpet. **Do** put it on a hard, flat surface like a table.
- **Do** make sure the fans aren't obstructed. **Don't** block it with books/files/fabrics.
- **Do** dust around the PC and the PC case itself regularly

Ultimately, you want to keep the inside of the computer dust free. Putting the PC on the floor means that when it's on, the fans are running and they are likely to suck up the dust and dirt from the floor putting it right inside the PC itself as it's working to cool down. Equally, blocking the ventilation system also means that it will struggle to get clean air and is more likely to suck dirt into the system as well as potentially overheating.

PUBLIC WI-FI SAFETY

Although it is very handy to connect to the free wifi in cafes and restaurants etc. be aware that there may be malicious users who are out to access your device and get access to your information. It is easy for them to intercept information or even replicate a wifi link.

Some tips:

- Make sure the wifi hotspot is a legitimate one and has the padlock symbol when connecting (SSL certificate)
- Avoid logging into any sites that require personal information (banking apps, social networking, online shopping)
- Make sure you have some kind of protection/antivirus on your device
- Consider using your mobile data as it should be more secure than public wifi as it acts as your own private network.
- Turn off file sharing on your device (such as Apple's AirDrop)
- Consider using a VPN (Virtual Private Network). There are third-party apps to help with this

VIRUSES

WHAT IS IT?

A computer virus is a piece of code designed to harm the computer or data on it. It is very similar to a human virus in that it travels from host to host and can duplicate itself. Viruses can corrupt your computer and cause detrimental effects such as losing important documents and information. What's worse, is they can remain dormant and not show any signs of being there so you may never know.

SAFETY TIPS

Make sure you have some kind of antivirus installed whether it is free or paid for.

Don't have more than one activated as they can conflict with each other. There are many good and free antivirus software available such as AVG, please contact us for more advice on this if you wish to know which ones we would recommend at the time.

Keep all your software up to date so that there are fewer loopholes for the virus to get in through.

Make use of your Windows firewall which should automatically be on your laptop or PC. If you are more confident, play with some of the advanced settings but if not, just make sure it is activated. This can be accessed on the control panel.

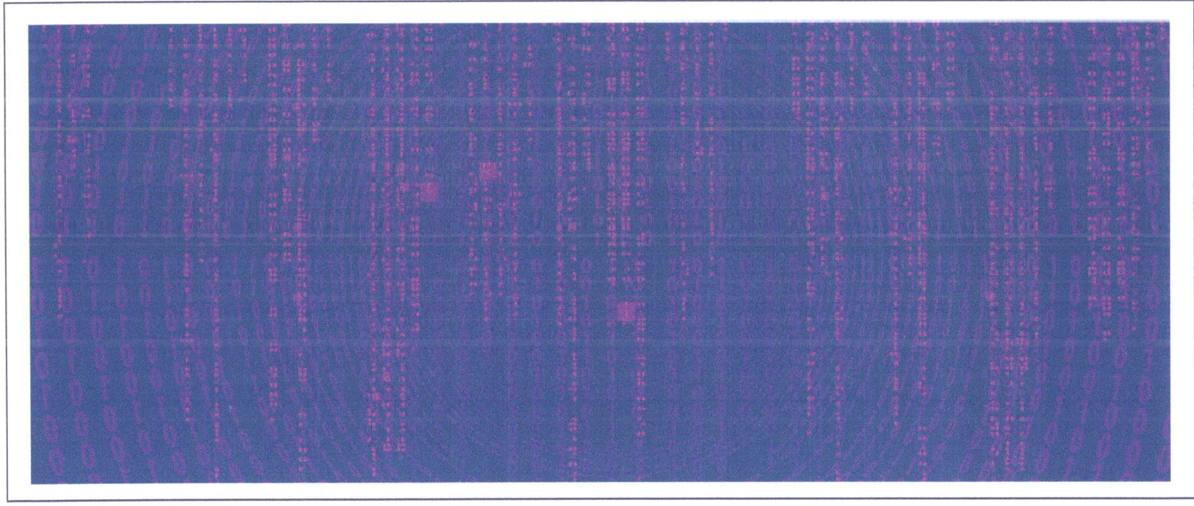

MALWARE

WHAT IS IT?

Malware (malicious software) is any type of software that is intended to harm your computer. This includes viruses, spyware, worms, etc. They can be designed to do a variety of bad things including locking your data from you, stealing information, corrupting your computer, and controlling your computer.

SAFETY TIPS

Similar tips as with protection from viruses. Make sure your software is up to date and your antivirus is installed and active. Don't click on any suspicious links as they may download the software onto your computer. Make sure you use a strong password for your device to stop people from managing to gain access and remotely control it.

SPAM

WHAT IS IT?

Spam is messages sent via the internet that are usually sent to a large number of people either in an attempt to advertise or trick people into providing their details. Spam can be sent from legitimate companies for advertising purposes and should allow the user to unsubscribe. There are the types of spam, however, that are sent with malicious intent and pretend that there is some action that you need to take.

SAFETY TIPS

Similar tips as with protection from viruses. Make sure your software is up to date and your antivirus is installed and active. Don't click on any suspicious links as they may download the software onto your computer. Make sure you use a strong password for your device to stop people from managing to gain access and remotely control it. Applying spam filters to your email may be helpful but it can be confusing and some will continue to get through. Equally, it can block legitimate emails.

There are other tips that will help you avoid downloading any malware through spam emails. Firstly, check who the email is sent to. Many spam emails won't have been sent to your actual email address so if you don't see it there, assume it's spam. Secondly, check the actual email address of who it's from.

Many emails that are spam look like they are from a legitimate person or company as they set their display name but if you look at their actual email address, it's usually a random address unrelated to the name it's displaying. Also, if there are any links in an email that look suspicious, don't click them.

Any information that you need to access will be easy for you to get hold of online whether it's just a website or your account information (i.e. someone may say you've been charged for an order when you haven't ordered anything but don't panic).

You can copy and paste the email address into an online email checker to see if it is trustworthy or not. Please contact us if you would like advice on which website to use for checking the validity of an email address.

PASSWORDS

We are coming to a time where passwords are crucial in almost everything we do. They need to be complex enough to stop people from being able to easily guess them but easy enough for us to remember. Many sites have lots of requirements of what needs to be included making it more difficult. We are supposed to change them regularly to keep it secure but that's a lot of hassle.

Here's what you're supposed to do:
- Have a password that is at least 12 characters long
- Do not use any obvious words in the password (such as your birthday, name, your pet's name, etc.)
- Have upper case characters, lower case characters, numbers, and symbols
- Change it every 3 months
- Do not write them down anywhere
- Don't tell anybody your password

All of this seems simple enough but it's incredibly difficult to apply in your everyday life. First, I'll give some ideas of what you can do to make this easier, and then some tips about realistic ways to get close to the aforementioned rules.

PASSWORD MANAGER

Using one of these will store all of your passwords so really, you only need to come up with one. However, this one has to be incredibly strong as you don't want anybody to guess it, otherwise, they will have access to all of your other passwords. This can then be the password that you apply the above rules to.

BOOK OF PASSWORDS

This is one of the classical nono's of password security. If you write down your password then anybody can have access to it. However, this one may not be so bad if you keep the passwords somewhere safe at home in a locked drawer. And you could use your own code to indicate which password is for which website. It is unlikely that anybody will come into your house and take your password book. Please note though, keeping a password book is officially ill-advised.

PASSWORDS

The easiest way to generate a password is to use some kind of memorable information but scramble it with symbols and numbers. For example, if you love roses you could have a password of 'I love roses' and change it to '!_l0v3_rose5#' which is 13 characters long. It may seem complicated but once you figure out what logic you wish to apply, it'll be easy to remember but difficult for others to guess. Another way would be to look around your desk (if you sit at one when using your computer) and pick three objects left to right. For example, you could use ' ruler_holepunch_pens07 ' which is a long password, but as long as the items stay in the same place on your desk, you won't have too much trouble remembering it.

1. Click 'File' at the top left

2. Make sure 'Info' is selected from the left-hand side

3. Click on the dropdown under 'Permissions' section at the top

4. Select 'Encrypt with password'

5. Type in the password

6. Retype the password

7. Save document and close

8. Check that when you open it, it requires a password

Note: *Passwords are case-sensitive and cannot be recovered if lost.*

CONNECTING YOUR DEVICES

Most of us have one or more devices that we use at the same time. If you have a Desktop PC, you'll be using a mouse and keyboard. You may also want to use a microphone, speakers and perhaps even other devices like a graphics tablet. The good news is, most devices are now 'plug and play' which means that you don't need to do any hard work in order to be able to use them. The drivers will be automatically downloaded and your PC should be able to recognise what kind of device is connected.

However, there are times when it can go a bit wrong. During the installation process, say for a printer, it may not be able to connect properly. Once something is installed but not working properly, it can be a little more problematic.

Option 1: Uninstall and then reinstall. That just means you have a chance to go through the steps again and that usually works in the majority of cases.

Option 2: Troubleshooting. You go through the settings and see what devices are connected. From there, you may have the option to troubleshoot a particular device. When things aren't working properly on a PC, there will usually be an error code or a specific warning. Typing that code into Google and the device you're trying to connect may end up showing you various online forums where people may have experienced similar issues. From other people's experiences, you may be able to find assistance.

Mostly, wired devices don't really go wrong with connections these days. If they do, it's usually because of the cable itself. Wireless connections can cause more chaos. One of the reasons can be to do with which frequency your devices are connected to (i.e. 2.4 GHz, 5 GHz, and 6 GHz). If they aren't on the same channel, they won't be able to connect. There can be issues with bandwidth or different components within the device. Either way, there's more room for things to go wrong.

TROUBLESHOOTING WIRELESS CONNECTIONS:

- Make sure you're connected to the same network if using WiFi. It seems obvious but say for example you've got a range extender, it may be that one device is connected to that and the other is connected to the router itself.

- Make sure the device is discoverable (not hidden). Security settings allow you to make a device hidden which means it won't be visible to other devices. That's great if you're in a public setting but not great when you are trying to connect to your own PC.

- If you're using Bluetooth, again, make sure Bluetooth is on and discoverable for both devices. For some devices (such as speakers) you may have to press and hold a button to allow it to search for devices to connect to.

REMOVING EXTERNAL DRIVES

Whenever you plug in an external hard drive, your PC is reading it for information. A lot of people just pull it out when they are done, but that can lead to corruption, especially if files are open and being read from it. To avoid this, it's always best to eject the hard drive first. There are two ways to do this.

Option 1:
File Explorer -> This PC -> Right-click on the external drive and select Eject

Option 2:
Bottom Right Corner of the Taskbar there should be an icon for the USB drive, if not select the arrow to show hidden icons. Hover over the various icons until you find the USB drive, right-click and eject.
If your drive is corrupted when you plug it in, a notification will come up and it should give you the option to 'scan and repair'.

TROUBLESHOOTING

Naturally, the biggest problem we have with technology is when things aren't working how we want them to. This is where troubleshooting is. Not all of us have an IT company ready to help us at any time of day with our questions. The best option is to help ourselves. Here are the basic steps I would suggest if things aren't going how you expect them to:

- Turn the device off and on again
- Unplug the device and plug it back in
- Make sure all the connections seem stable (no loose inputs)
- Check the internet connection
- Google the device and the error
- Make sure you're not overloading the device with requests (i.e. having too many tabs open)
- Check if it works elsewhere. Say you're using a USB stick that's not reading properly on a PC, try plugging it into a different one and see if you experience the same issue. If you're having a problem with a laptop working properly, plug it in to see if it performs better or use it elsewhere to see if it is the internet connection. The main goal is to find out the source of the problem. When you have multiple devices talking to one another, it could be any of them.

Ultimately, research is your best friend. A lot of technical products come with a manual and there will be a troubleshooting section within that. That's the best place to start if this quick help doesn't offer a solution. Secondly, using an online search engine to find solutions often proves the quickest way if there is a technical fault. If you don't get any relevant results, then it is likely to be an issue elsewhere rather than that specific product.

INSTALLING SOFTWARE

Whenever you get a new piece of technology, there will always be software to install whether on the device itself or on the device you are connecting to. Certain products (like a graphics tablet) will need certain drivers to be installed in order to function properly. The good news is, most software will automatically be installed when it is a 'plug and play' device. However, there are instances where this doesn't happen.

If you have a device that you need to install software for, the best option is to go to the manufacturer's website and select the 'download software' option. If it isn't obvious on their website, type in the manufacturer's name, device and 'download software' into a search engine. When you navigate to the 'download software/drivers' page, there will likely be an input box where you can type in the model/serial number of your device and that will guide you to what software you need to download and install. From there, you follow the on-screen instructions.

Of course, there will be software that you want to use on a device. The most important part to check is 'system requirements'. This ensures that your PC can run the software and not crash. However, there are times when you will meet the system requirements, but that doesn't mean it will run properly. It's worth doing a little bit of research into the program that you are looking to install to see what other users recommend. This does mostly go for creative software such as video editors, as they require the most powerful PCs.

There are other pieces of software (such as antivirus) that will clash, so again, make sure to keep an eye on what you already have installed to avoid any conflicts that may arise. Say, for example, you want to use Adobe Edge and Adobe Premiere Pro at the same time. Your PC may be able to handle one without much problem but trying to run both at the same time can prove too much.

If your PC is slowing down or struggling, open up the task manager to see what is using up the majority of your RAM. That will give you an indication of whether one particular piece of software is the problem or if there are just too many tasks going on simultaneously.

FREE CREATIVE SOFTWARE

In the age where social media is so prevalent, and there is a large need for digital content (even from print), it helps to know where you can start. There are a lot of paid software packages available (such as Adobe Creative Cloud) but these can get very expensive.

The good news is, there are so many free options that you can use to create high-quality digital content for free, providing that you either have a laptop, tablet or smartphone. Whatever type of content you need, there should be free software out there that will suit those needs.

PHOTOGRAPHY

PHOTOPEA

We have all heard of Adobe Photoshop but wouldn't it be great if there was a free version that could do basically all of the same things? Well, that's exactly what Photopea does. It's a web-based application that has pretty much all the same tools as Photoshop and although it may not have the latest updates, it can definitely edit photographs to a high standard.

Not only is it great for editing photographs but it can also be used to create digital content from scratch and even comes with templates!

The only real downside is that it can crash from time to time and it's difficult to create a good workflow. Every time you save the file, it will download a new version rather than saving over the last one.

DARKTABLE

This was the software that I found most favourable for editing RAW image files. It's comparable to Lightroom and it's not an intensive application. There aren't as many features as Photopea but if you want to edit RAW directly and process the curves of the image, this is a fantastic option.

GIMP

Another fantastic photo editing tool, similar to Photoshop. It allows you to work in layers, edit RAW files and a whole host of other things. It's free to download. It has a less friendly user interface than some of the other options out there, but it can definitely help with creating and editing high-quality digital content.

OTHER TOOLS

DAVINCI RESOLVE

A fantastic video editor that has a free version and a paid version. A lot of famous films have been edited using Davinci Resolve (Avatar, Deadpool 2, Pirates of the Caribbean and Bohemian Rapsody to name but a few) so it's a fantastic platform. It's also great because it's less processor-intensive than options like Premiere Pro. It is more reliant on the graphics processing unit so can be a better option for many.

It has a great workflow starting with the cutting, to the editing and then adding in special effects, finishing with the music and sound levels. You can navigate between sections easily and there are a lot of tutorials on the internet to help you achieve whatever you are looking to do.

CANVA

Most people have heard of Canva at this point as it is a fantastic web-based application for creating any kind of digital content. You can create things ready for print and it has so many template designs from things like logos all the way through to Instagram Reels. They offer a huge library of elements (graphics, photos, videos) that you can use for free in your materials. If you wish to access more, you can upgrade to the premium version.

WIX

There are many web-based applications that are drag-and-drop tools for building a website but Wix is a fantastic option all around for businesses. They not only allow you to buy a domain and set up a website, but they also offer a whole load of applications to help you run your business as effectively as possible. If you want bookings, they can help with that and if you want to run virtual events, there's also an app for that! You can offer subscriptions, and loyalty programs, and host an online shop.

What's even more fantastic than that are the tools they offer outside of the website. You can manage your invoices, quotations, inbox, etc. all from the Wix website. You can view your analytics for your website and also your finances. All of that costs though. But you can create and publish a website for free and only upgrade once your business is bringing in money.

OTHER TOOLS

CLICKUP

This is one of the best free online tools to use for project management for individuals and small companies. As with most similar software, it enables you to create your to-do list and break those items down into smaller tasks.

As well as that, you have the ability to create different media types within the app. You can record voice clips, and create written documents but you also can create 'whiteboards'. These are perfect for creating flow charts or organisational structure charts.

There is the option to create calendar events and assign due dates for each of your tasks. You can then share your workspace with other team members so that projects are collaborative.

GANTT CHARTS

Gantt charts are another great tool for project management. You have your overall project timeline and your various tasks that will allow for project completion. Each task goes on a separate line and then a certain amount of time is allocated for each task (and is usually colour-coded).

As it's a popular tool, there are a number of paid and free options so it depends on your design preference.

onlinegantt.com is a free option that requires no registration. smartsheet.com has both paid and free options.

UNSPLASH/PEXELS

One of the biggest hurdles when creating using technology is photography or videography. Not everyone is fortunate enough to be able to hire a professional which is why we are fortunate to have a lot of royalty-free materials available.

For photographs, Unsplash is a great option, especially if you are just looking for photographs to accompany a presentation or video. Ideally, credit the photographers for their work but the fantastic thing is that there are so many options.

For using snippets of videos in your main video, or on your website, you can use Pexels. They also do photographs but their videos are fantastic quality and cover a variety of topics.

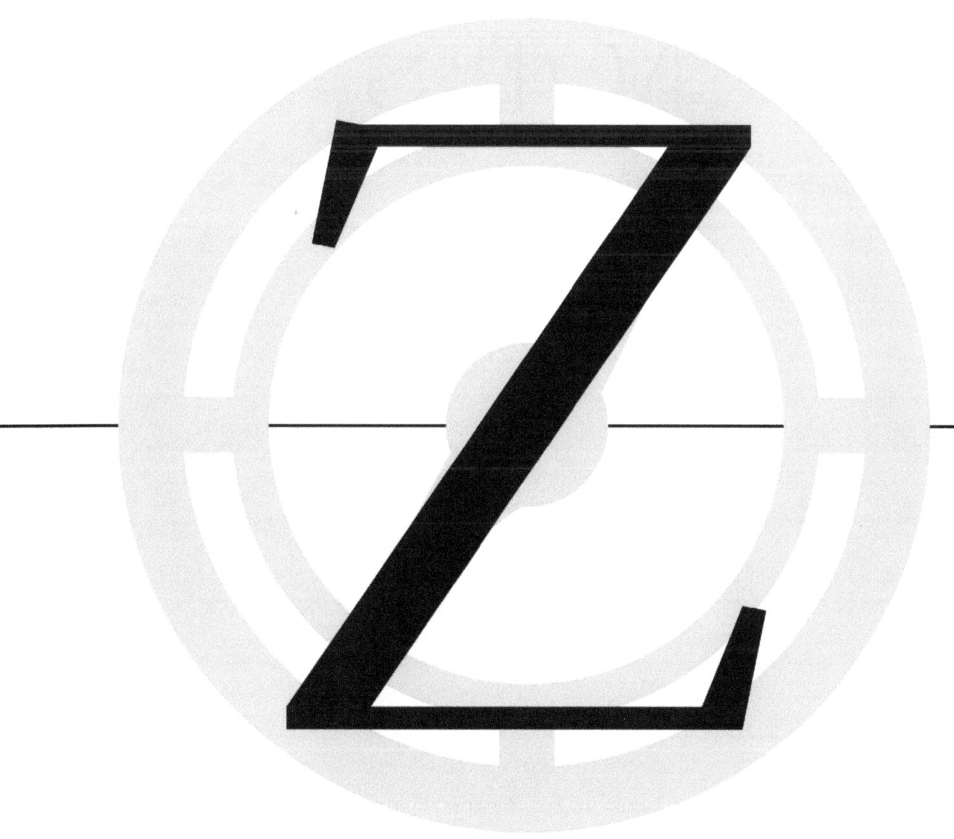

CONCLUSION

PCs stand for personal computers for a reason. They offer a personalised experience. Everyone has a different way of working, with various sets of needs and computers have the capacity to adapt in almost any way their user sees fit. We all want to use different tools and prefer different looks. It all fits into the user experience.

We live in an ever-changing world and technology is always evolving and it can be a daunting task to try and keep up with it.

This guide was designed to help any person who wants a breakdown of certain terminology or quick assistance with certain technological problems. We all have moments where we aren't sure what's gone wrong and it can create a sense of panic. There isn't always someone to call, but the more we understand, the easier it is to find a solution.

The next few pages are left so that you can make any notes in relation to your personal experience with PCs or any shortcuts/information that you want handy to you when working. I hope you have found this guide helpful and that it has increased your confidence when using computers.

NOTES

NOTES

NOTES

NOTES

NOTES

NOTES